D1614106

WORLD'S BIGGEST

TITANIC Trucks

by Meish Goldish

Consultant: James Acock
Heavy Vehicle Specialist
D & A Consultants, Inc.

BEARPORT
PUBLISHING

New York, New York

Credits

Cover and Title Page, © Fernando Rodrigues/Shutterstock; TOC, © R. Gino Santa Maria/Shutterstock; 4, Courtesy of The Midnight Rider; 5, Courtesy of The Midnight Rider; 6, © Robert Pernell/BigStockPhoto.com; 7, © AP Images/Charles Bennett; 8, © Darinburt/iStockphoto; 9, © Trevor Smithers/ARPS/Alamy; 10, © Robert Pernell/Shutterstock; 11, © William Caram/Alamy; 12, © J. Hanson/Newspix/News Ltd; 13, © Jean-Marc La Roque/Auscape; 14-15, © Dick Blume/The Syracuse Newspapers; 16, Courtesy of NASA Kennedy Space Center; 17, Courtesy of NASA Kennedy Space Center; 18, © UPI Photo/Stephanie Krell/Landov; 19, Courtesy of BIGFOOT 4X4, Inc.; 20, © Ray Wert/Jalopnik.com; 21, © Ray Wert/Jalopnik.com; 22TL, © Bram van Broekhoven/Shutterstock; 22TR, © ownway/shutterstock; 22BL, © Storyguy/fotolia; 22BR, © Creatas/Photolibrary; 23A, © egd/shutterstock; 23B, © Barry Salmons/Shutterstock; 23C, © Marek Slusarczyk/Shutterstock; 23D, © Sindre Ellingsen/Alamy; 23E, © F1online/digitale Bildagentur/GmbH/Alamy; 23F, © Mike Clarke/iStockphoto; 23G, © Daniel Loiselle/iStockphoto.

Publisher: Kenn Goin
Editorial Director: Adam Siegel
Creative Director: Spencer Brinker
Photo Researcher: Omni-Photo Communications, Inc.
Design: Debrah Kaiser

Library of Congress Cataloging-in-Publication Data

Goldish, Meish.
  Titanic trucks / by Meish Goldish.
      p. cm. — (World's biggest)
  Includes bibliographical references and index.
  ISBN-13: 978-1-59716-957-8 (library binding)
  ISBN-10: 1-59716-957-9 (library binding)
  1. Trucks—Juvenile literature. I. Title.

  TL230.15.G65 2010
  629.224—dc22
                                        2009006706

For more information, write to Bearport Publishing Company, Inc., 101 Fifth Avenue, Suite 6R, New York, New York 10003. Printed in the United States of America in North Mankato, Minnesota.

122009
120109CG

10 9 8 7 6 5 4 3 2

CONTENTS

THE MIDNIGHT RIDER

Length: 70 feet (21.3 m)   **Width:** 8 feet, 5 inches (2.6 m)

Height: 13 feet, 8 inches (4.2 m)   **Weight:** 50,560 pounds (22,934 kg)

Many people like to ride in long, fancy cars called **limousines**. Yet in Las Vegas and Southern California, some people prefer a fancy truck—The Midnight Rider! This huge **tractor trailer** is the largest limousine in the world. People rent it for parties. The giant truck holds up to 40 passengers. They can watch movies and enjoy food as they ride in style.

The Midnight Rider is made for having fun. Yet most huge trucks are built to do work—and not small jobs. As you'll soon see, big trucks are used for carrying big loads.

tractor

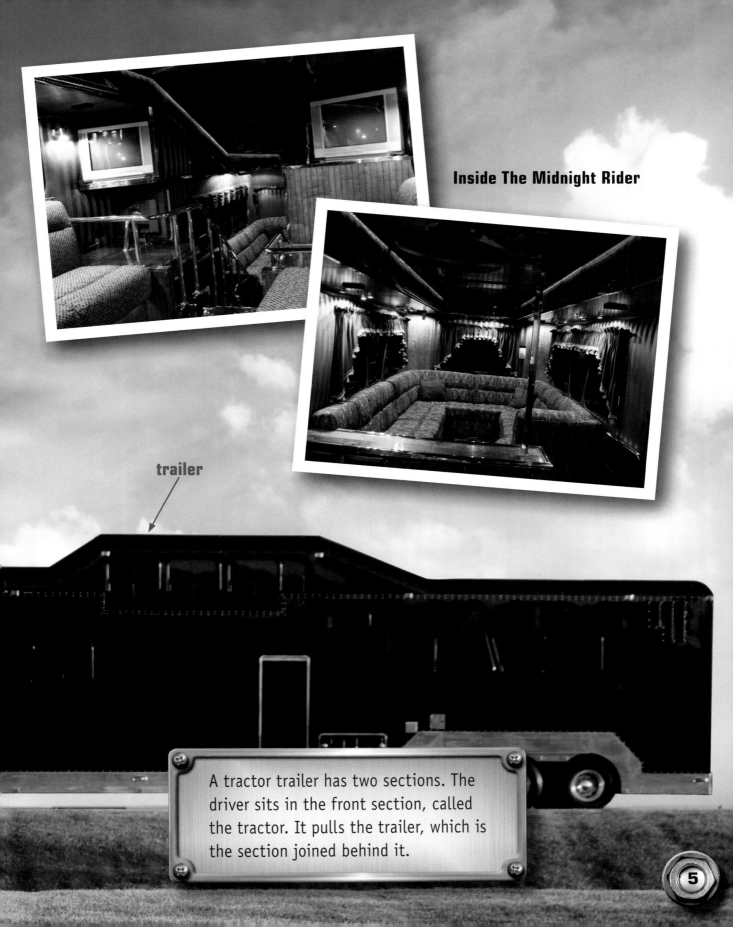

Inside The Midnight Rider

trailer

A tractor trailer has two sections. The driver sits in the front section, called the tractor. It pulls the trailer, which is the section joined behind it.

CAR CARRIER

Length: 70 feet (21.3 m)

Height: 13 feet, 6 inches (4.1 m)

Width: 8 feet, 6 inches (2.6 m)

Maximum Weight: 80,000 pounds (36,287 kg)

After cars are built in a factory, they need to be delivered to the showroom where people can buy them. The new cars can't be driven there because then they would be "used" cars. So how do they get to the customers? Some of the cars are placed on huge tractor trailers, called car carriers, that bring the cars to the places where they will be sold.

To load a truck, each car is driven up a ramp. The truck's upper deck, or level, is filled first. Then the cars are placed on the lower deck. Strong cords and chains hold them in place so they don't fall off the truck as they travel.

A tractor trailer can hold up to 12 small-size cars.

LOGGING TRUCK

Length: 70 feet (21.3 m)

Height: 13 feet, 6 inches (4.1 m)

Width: 8 feet, 6 inches (2.6 m)

Maximum Weight: 80,000 pounds (36,287 kg)

A logging truck is a kind of tractor trailer—with a twist. It doesn't have any sides. Instead, the back section is a pole trailer where long, heavy trees that have been cut down in the forest can be loaded. Strong chains or cords are used to hold the logs in place. The truck then brings the logs to factories where the wood is used to make furniture, paper, and other products.

pole trailer

Some logging trucks can carry 55,000 pounds (24,948 kg) of wood. That's about the same weight as five elephants!

TANKER

Length: 70 feet (21.3 m)   **Width:** 8 feet, 6 inches (2.6 m)

Height: 13 feet, 6 inches (4.1 m)   **Maximum Weight:** 80,000 pounds (36,287 kg)

Tractor trailers don't just carry goods like cars and logs that can be tied down. A **tanker** is a kind of tractor trailer that carries a liquid, such as gasoline, orange juice, or milk. The liquid is stored in a long, round steel tank. It can hold up to 9,000 gallons (34,069 l). That's enough liquid to fill 72,000 pint-size cartons of milk!

Some tankers carry more than one kind of liquid on the same trip. The inside of the tank is divided into sections in order to keep the different liquids separate from one another.

A tanker carrying oil

Some tanks are refrigerated so that liquids such as orange juice stay cool and don't spoil.

ROAD TRAIN

Length: 175 feet, 6 inches (53.5 m) (for a three-trailer train)

Height: 14 feet (4.3 m)

Width: 8 feet, 3 inches (2.5 m)

Some trucks need to carry such a big load that everything can't fit in just one trailer. How do people solve this problem? They attach more trailers to the back of the truck, which makes it look like a train. In fact, this kind of truck is called a **road train**.

Road trains are found mainly in Australia. They travel between cities that are very far apart. The extra-long trucks stay on roads that are mostly straight and flat and have little traffic. The trains are too big to pull into cities. Instead, they unload their goods at special road train stations that are located outside cities.

The longest road train on record was created in 2006 in Australia. It had 112 trailers and stretched 4,837 feet (1.47 km)—almost a mile long!

12

SNOWPLOW

Width of Syracuse Snowplow Blade:
32 feet, 3 inches (9.8 m)

Height of Syracuse Snowplow Blade:
4 feet (1.2 m)

Snowy weather is beautiful, but it can also be dangerous. Towns and cities need to make sure their streets are clean and safe for people to drive on. To remove snow, people drive trucks called snowplows that push the snow to the side of the road.

Some cities get only a few inches of snow each winter. Others, like Syracuse, New York, get more than 9 feet (2.7 m). In fact, Syracuse is one of the snowiest cities in the United States. So it's not a surprise that they have the biggest snowplow in the world. The blade on this truck is 32 feet, 3 inches (9.8 m) wide and 4 feet (1.2 m) high. It is used to clear the mounds of snow that pile up at the Syracuse airport.

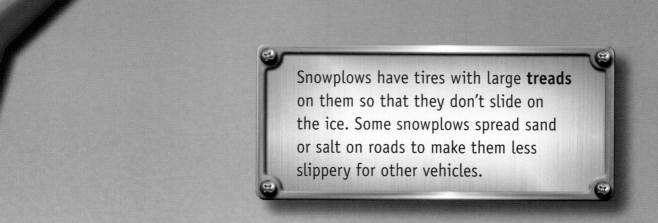

Snowplows have tires with large **treads** on them so that they don't slide on the ice. Some snowplows spread sand or salt on roads to make them less slippery for other vehicles.

The Syracuse snowplow

CRAWLER-TRANSPORTER

Length: 131 feet (40 m) **Width:** 114 feet (35 m)

Height: 26 feet (8 m) **Weight:** 6 million pounds (2,722 metric tons)

A space shuttle can weigh as much as 171,000 pounds (77,564 kg). Yet it is still able to blast off into the sky. One thing it can't do, however, is move on land. Is there a truck big enough—and strong enough—to carry one? Yes! At the Kennedy Space Center in Florida, a crawler-transporter is used to move a space shuttle to its launch pad.

The space shuttle is placed on top of the crawler-transporter's giant platform, which is about the same size as a baseball diamond. The crawler-transporter weighs six million pounds (2,722 metric tons)—without the space shuttle on board! With its heavy load, the truck moves only one mile per hour (1.6 kph). No wonder it's called a crawler!

The space shuttle
Discovery

The Kennedy Space Center has
two crawler-transporters. They
are named Hans and Franz.

MONSTER TRUCK

Height: 10–12 feet, 6 inches (3–3.8 m)

Average Width: 12 feet, 6 inches (3.8 m)

Weight: 9,500–13,000 pounds (4,309–5,897 kg)

Some trucks aren't just big—they're monsters! A **monster truck** is a **pickup truck** with oversize wheels and a powerful engine. Most monster trucks are about 12 feet (3.7 m) high.

Unlike most other trucks, monster trucks don't do work. Instead, their job is to entertain. At monster truck rallies, crowds of people watch the drivers race the giant trucks in the mud and crush old cars by riding on top of them. Some drivers even do tricks with their huge vehicles, such as speeding around on just two wheels.

Weighing 28,000 pounds (12,701 kg) and standing more than 15 feet (4.6 m) tall, Bigfoot 5 is the heaviest and tallest pickup truck in the world.

Bigfoot 5

MONSTER FIRE TRUCK

Length: 38 feet (11.6 m)   **Width:** 12 feet, 4 inches (3.8 m)
Height: 11 feet, 9.5 inches (3.6 m)   **Weight:** 35,000 pounds (15,876 kg)

Most monster trucks are driven at rallies where they race each other, crush cars, and do tricks. Yet the longest monster truck of all isn't used at races. Instead, it is used to help save lives.

Big Red is a monster fire truck. Built in 1937, it first served as a real fire truck in Kentucky. After many years of helping to put out fires, the truck was retired. Later, its tires were replaced with much larger ones to turn it into a monster fire truck. Today, Big Red is shown at parades, fairs, and other events to raise money for children who are very ill. After more than 70 years, Big Red is still doing its part to help make people's lives better.

Big Red holds the Guinness World Record for being the longest and heaviest monster truck in the world.

A concrete mixer carries cement, sand, gravel, and water to a construction site. The tank on the truck spins the mixture to make concrete that is used for sidewalks and buildings. The tank can hold about 20 tons (18 metric tons) of concrete.

A truck with a mobile crane lifts heavy items at a construction site. Some of these giant cranes can lift 550 tons (499 metric tons)—the same weight as about 350 cars.

A garbage truck collects trash and drives it to a dump site. Some of these trucks hold up to 14 tons (12.7 metric tons) of trash and can collect garbage from more than 800 homes before they have to be emptied.

Tow trucks are strong enough to pull out cars and other vehicles that are stuck in the snow or mud. They can also remove vehicles that have broken down on the road.

GLOSSARY

limousines (LIM-uh-*zeenz*) long, fancy cars

monster truck (MON-stur TRUHK) a pickup truck with oversize wheels that is used for racing and doing stunts at shows

pickup truck (PIK-up TRUHK) a light truck with an open body and low sides

road train (ROHD TRAYN) a truck that has two or more trailers attached to its tractor

tanker (TANG-kur) a truck with a large tank that carries a liquid such as gasoline, oil, or milk

tractor trailer (TRAK-tur TRAYL-ur) a truck with two sections; the front section, called the tractor, pulls the rear section, called the trailer

treads (TREDZ) ridges on a truck's tires that help stop it from sliding

INDEX

BIBLIOGRAPHY

Federal Size Regulations for Commercial Motor Vehicles. Washington, D.C.: U.S. Department of Transportation Federal Highway Administration (Oct. 2004). (http://ops.fhwa.dot.gov/freight/publications/size_regs_final_rpt/)

Gerew, Gary, and Stan Linhorst. "Syracuse Has the Biggest Snow Plow in the World." Syracuse OnLine. (www.syracuse.com/weather/snow/stories/)

www.allabouttrucks.com

www.bigfoot4x4.com/history.html

www.shawbros.com/site/index.php?info_id=111

www.themidnightrider.com

READ MORE

Bingham, Caroline. *Big Rig.* New York: Dorling Kindersley (2000).

Kalman, Bobbie, and Reagan Miller. *Tough Trucks.* New York: Crabtree Publishing (2007).

Morganelli, Adrianna. *Trucks: Pickups to Big Rigs.* New York: Crabtree Publishing (2007).

Robbins, Ken. *Trucks: Giants of the Highway.* New York: Aladdin (2002).

LEARN MORE ONLINE

To learn more about titanic trucks, visit
www.bearportpublishing.com/WorldsBiggest

ABOUT THE AUTHOR

Meish Goldish has written more than 200 books for children. He lives in Brooklyn, New York.